MRS T's BEDSIDE BOOK

Javelin Books
POOLE · DORSET

GIVE ME THE MOONLIGHT...
NK UP WITH US
LINK UP W
NATIONAL CAMPAIG
Link up w

First published in the UK 1985 by Javelin Books,
Link House, West Street, Poole, Dorset, BH15 1LL

Copyright © 1985 Blandford Press
Photographs: Popperfoto
Designed: Mike Ricketts
Picture selection & captions: J G (& colleagues)

British Library Cataloguing in Publication Data

Mrs. T.'s bedside book.
  1. Great Britain—Politics and government—
  1979——Anecdotes, facetiae, satire, etc.
  941.085'8'0207   DA592

  ISBN 0-7137-1708-4

The publisher accepts no responsibility for the state of the pound, Britain's decline as a world power, Ronald Reagan or anyone's lost MBE.

Coming soon: The Thin Edge of the Wedgie.
              Live and Let Di.

Printed in Great Britain by
R. J. Acford Ltd., Chichester, Sussex.